Two-Dad Families

by Connor Stratton

FOCUS READERS

BEACON

www.focusreaders.com

Focus Readers is distributed by North Star Editions:
sales@northstareditions.com | 888-417-0195

Produced for Focus Readers by Red Line Editorial.

Photographs ©: Shutterstock Images, cover, 1, 4, 7, 8, 10, 13, 14–15, 19, 21, 22, 25, 27, 29; iStockphoto, 16

Library of Congress Cataloging-in-Publication Data
Names: Stratton, Connor, author.
Title: Two-dad families / by Connor Stratton.
Description: Mendota Heights, MN: Focus Readers, [2025] | Series: All
  families | Includes index. | Audience term: Children | Audience: Grades
  2-3
Identifiers: LCCN 2024036030 (print) | LCCN 2024036031 (ebook) | ISBN
  9798889983941 (hardcover) | ISBN 9798889984221 (paperback) | ISBN
  9798889984771 (pdf) | ISBN 9798889984504 (ebook)
Subjects: LCSH: Gay fathers--Juvenile literature. | Gay fathers--Family
  relationships--Juvenile literature. | Gay pride celebrations--Juvenile
  literature.
Classification: LCC HQ76.13 .S78 2025 (print) | LCC HQ76.13 (ebook) | DDC
  306.874/208664--dc23/eng/20240911
LC record available at https://lccn.loc.gov/2024036030
LC ebook record available at https://lccn.loc.gov/2024036031

Printed in the United States of America
Mankato, MN
012025

About the Author

Connor Stratton writes and edits nonfiction children's books. He lives in Minnesota.

Table of Contents

Chapter 1

Father's Day at Pride

Today is Father's Day. So, a girl starts writing in a card. She describes what she loves about one of her fathers. Then the girl writes in another card. She writes to her other father.

Kids may add bright colors and decorations to Father's Day cards.

The girl gives the cards to her dads. They both give her a big hug. Then they all get ready. They go to a Pride parade. Pride Month celebrates the LGBTQ+ community.

At the parade, the girl skips. She holds hands with her dads. Thousands of others walk with

Did You Know?

June is Pride Month. Father's Day falls on the third Sunday of June.

 People often wave rainbow flags at Pride parades.

them. Many people wear bright colors. Some carry banners, too.

The girl loves to celebrate her dads. And she loves to honor what makes her family special.

Chapter 2

About Two-Dad Families

Two-dad families are part of the LGBTQ+ community. This community welcomes people across genders and **sexualities**. The letters stand for lesbian, gay, bisexual, transgender, and queer.

 About 8 percent of adults are part of the LGBTQ+ community.

The plus sign has a meaning, too. It shows the community is also home to many more **identities**.

Fathers in two-dad families may identify in different ways. Some identify as gay. This is a type of sexuality. Gay individuals are attracted to others of the same gender. Dads might also identify as bisexual, or bi. Bi people are attracted to more than one gender. Some dads are transgender, or trans. Trans people were **assigned** a different gender at birth.

Fathers may also identify as queer. A queer identity can describe gender or sexuality. It can also describe both. Some people might not fit neatly into other identities.

Identifying as queer lets them be who they are.

Two-dad families form in many ways. Adoption is one way. An adopted child has parents who are different from their **birth parents**.

Surrogacy is another way. This happens when two people cannot have a baby by themselves. So,

Did You Know?

One or both dads may be trans. Some trans dads gave birth to their babies.

Some parents ask friends or family members to be surrogates.

those two people get help. Another

adult carries the baby in their body.

That person gives birth to the baby.

Then, the two parents take care of

the child.

Adoption

Birth parents are not always able to raise a child. When that happens, other parents may adopt the child. An adoptive family forms. Many two-dad families are adoptive.

Kids in adoptive families may face moments that other kids do not. For example, family members may not have the same skin color. People might question whether they are actually a family. Kids may feel confused or upset. They may wonder if something's wrong. However, nothing is wrong. Adopted kids fully belong in their families.

Same-sex couples are more likely to adopt than opposite-sex couples are.

Chapter 3

Similar and Different

Two-dad families are similar to other families in many ways. They have parents who love their children. Families manage jobs, school, and time at home. They help out in their communities.

LGBTQ+ parents are often active in their children's education.

They also spend time with friends and other family members.

Sometimes, two-dad families face **stigma**. Some people believe **stereotypes** about LGBTQ+ people. They might believe two men shouldn't be together. Or people might think families should be a certain way. They might say kids need a mother to be raised well. None of these beliefs are true.

In fact, people of all genders are great parents. However, society has

 Children with two dads may face stigma from kids at school.

gender roles. This means people of certain genders are expected to behave in certain ways. For example, women are often expected to do more of the parenting work.

It is less expected for men to lead a household.

As a result, two-dad families might get stared at sometimes. Other times, people might treat them differently. This treatment is a type of discrimination. It often takes the form of **homophobia**. Kids in two-dad families may

Did You Know?

Gay marriage became legal throughout the United States in 2015.

It's okay to feel sad when people say hurtful things. Talking about it can often help.

hear homophobic statements themselves. Or they might see their parents get treated poorly. This treatment sometimes happens from friends. Kids may feel upset as a result. They may want to avoid time with their friends.

Chapter 4

Taking Pride

Sometimes, kids in two-dad families are treated unfairly. Kids may feel upset. They might feel angry or confused. As a result, kids' mental health may suffer.

 Sometimes, playing or exercising can help people work through their feelings.

They might feel anxiety. Or they may deal with **depression**.

All of these feelings are okay. They are normal. Even so, it's important to talk about it. Kids can express their feelings in a variety of ways.

Kids can talk to their parents. They can talk to trusted adults at school, too. Kids can tell adults if classmates are bullying them. Adults can help it stop. Kids can also check in with one another.

Students can speak with counselors. Kids can talk about what they're going through.

They can ask how others are feeling. This helps people feel more connected. They feel less alone.

Children with two dads may also have questions. For example, kids may ask about their birth parents.

They might ask about who carried them. Families can talk openly about these questions. Sometimes, kids want to meet these people. If possible, kids can learn more about where they come from.

Kids with two dads can feel proud. Their parents are brave and strong.

Did You Know?

Some schools have LGBTQ+ groups. They support students in the LGBTQ+ community.

 LGBTQ+ groups can give students a space to talk about their identities.

Despite stigma, they formed caring families. They may be different from some other families. But they take pride in what makes them different. They are as joyful, safe, and loving as any other family.

FOCUS ON
Two-Dad Families

Write your answers on a separate piece of paper.

1. Write a paragraph explaining the main ideas of Chapter 3.

2. What are some ways your family is similar to and different from other families?

3. What does the T in LGBTQ+ stand for?
    A. two
    B. treatment
    C. transgender

4. Why can kids in two-dad families feel proud?
    A. Their parents took brave steps to form loving families.
    B. Their families never feel upset about mistreatment.
    C. Their families are the same as all other families.

5. What does **discrimination** mean in this book?

*Other times, people might treat them differently. This treatment is a type of **discrimination**. It often takes the form of homophobia.*

   A. taking actions to become more similar to others

   B. the forming of a new family through adoption

   C. mistreatment of others because of who they are

6. What does **mental health** mean in this book?

*They might feel angry or confused. As a result, kids' **mental health** may suffer.*

   A. how well or unwell someone's family is

   B. how well or unwell someone's mind and emotions are

   C. how well or unwell someone does in school

Answer key on page 32.

Glossary

assigned
Selected by an adult, often by a doctor.

birth parents
The first parents of a person who is adopted.

depression
A medical condition of deep, long-lasting sadness or loss of interest.

homophobia
Hatred or mistreatment of people because of their sexuality.

identities
The traits, labels, and beliefs that people use to define themselves.

sexualities
Identities that describe who people are attracted to or want to fall in love with.

stereotypes
Overly simple and harmful ideas of how all members of a certain group are.

stigma
Unfair and harmful ideas that a large group of people have about something.

To Learn More

BOOKS

Johnson, Chelsea, LaToya Council, and Carolyn Choi. *Love Without Bounds: An IntersectionAllies Book About Families*. New York: Dottir Press, 2023.

Lombardo, Jennifer. *The Story of the LGBTQ+ Rights Movement*. Buffalo, NY: Cavendish Square Publishing, 2024.

Prager, Sarah. *A Child's Introduction to Pride: The Inspirational History and Culture of the LGBTQIA+ Community*. New York: Black Dog & Leventhal, 2023.

NOTE TO EDUCATORS

Visit **www.focusreaders.com** to find lesson plans, activities, links, and other resources related to this title.

Index

Answer Key: 1. Answers will vary; **2.** Answers will vary; **3.** C; **4.** A; **5.** C; **6.** B